FABULOUS FRISBEE®

FABULOUS FRISBEE ®

by Dorothy Childers Schmitz

"FRISBEE" is a registered trademark of Wham-O-Mfg. Co., San Gabriel, Calitornia, U. S. Trademark Registration Number 679,186, issued May 26, 1959, for flying saucers used in sports games.

Library of Congress Catalog Card Number: 78-7416   Reprinted 1978

International Standard Book Numbers:
0-913940-88-7 Library Bound
0-89686-009-4

Edited by - Dr. Howard Schroeder
Prof. in Reading and Language Arts
Dept. of Elementary Education
Mankato State University

Gail McColl

CIP

Library of Congress
Cataloging in Publication Data

Schmitz, Dorothy Childers.
 Fabulous Frisbee.®

 (Funseekers)
 SUMMARY: The history and techniques of disc flying, the
national sport that began by tossing an empty pie plate.
 1. Disc Flying (Game) -- Juvenile literature.
 (1. Disc Flying (Game) I. Title.
GV1097.F7S35   796.2   78-7416
ISBN 0-913940-88-7

   A special thanks to Mr. Dan "Stork" Roddick and the International Frisbee®
Association, who supplied many necessary photos.

PHOTO CREDITS

International Frisbee® Association: Cover, 3, 5, 7, 9, 19, 21, 24A, 24B, 26,
       27, 28, 29, 31, 32
Mark E. Ahlstrom: 11, 12A, 12B, 13A, 13B, 14A, 15A, 15B, 15C, 16, 17A,
       17B, 23A, 23B

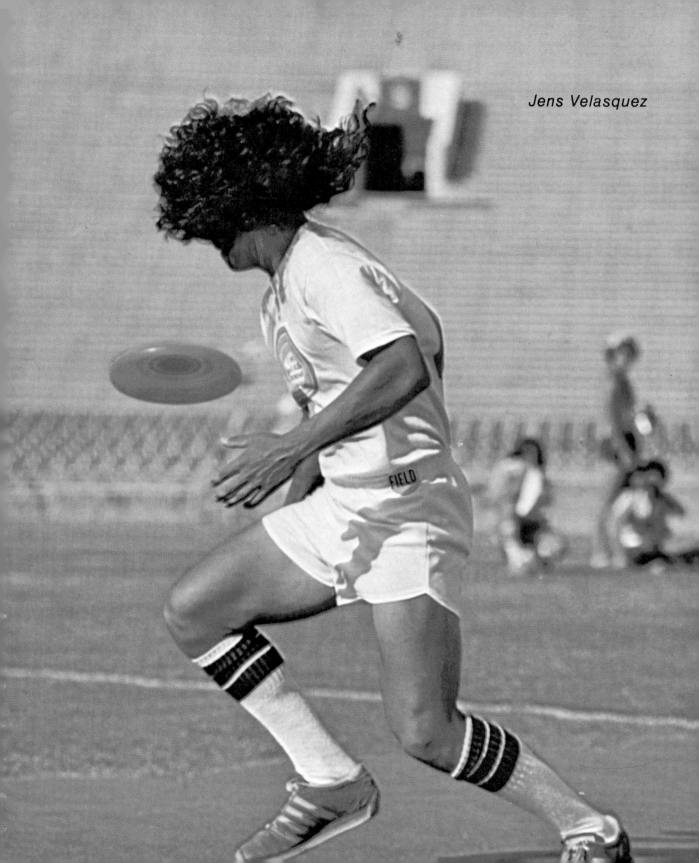

FABULOUS FRISBEE®

It's a great day for a walk in the park. There isn't a cloud in the sky. But wait! There is something in the sky. Just above the trees there is a round object hovering. There's another one! We're being invaded! What is this? They're all over the place! There's a red one, now a blue one, all colors. The yellow one is going back in the direction from which it came. I'm getting out of here! I thought this was a nice, peaceful park. This is weird! What's this? A sign on the tree says, **"FRISBEE® TOURNAMENT TODAY. COME AND BRING YOUR FRISBEE."**

It all began with a pie plate. Somebody discovered that after the pie was gone, it was fun to toss around the pie tin. Anybody could play. You didn't have to be tall, strong, or a certain age. All you needed was a yard in which to run and an empty pie tin. This was the beginning of a type of fun that has become a national sport.

There are all kinds of stories about the beginnings of the Frisbee®. Most of the stories agree that the name Frisbee came from the name of the pie company, Frisbie Pie Company in Bridgeport, Connecticut.

Not everyone tosses around a pie tin today. That's another story. During the time when many things were being made of plastic, someone decided that Frisbee® discs would be better made of plastic, too. The Wham-O-Company in California came up with a recipe for a plastic disc which was almost impossible to break. This company first changed the spelling from Frisbie to Frisbee and trademarked the name on their discs.

Sometime during the fifties, people began to get serious about their disc fun. It was still fun, and still a game, but they began to see the idea of tournaments and contests as a way to have even more fun. It would involve many people, a little competition, and a lot of excitement. This was the beginning of contests.

During the sixties, the International Frisbee Association was founded, and contests were held in many parts of our country. There were more contests started in California than anywhere else since that's the area the sport really began. By the late sixties, people of different ages throughout the country were enjoying tossing around the plastic discs, even if they had never heard of a tournament or contest.

Today, there are many kinds of contests in every part of the country. There are 100-yard distance throws, trick throwing, team games, and other kinds of competition to determine a national male and female champion.

Doug Corea

9

Whether you decide to become a national Frisbee® champion or just have fun in your own back yard, you will need to start with the basics. Anyone can throw a Frisbee disc, but it takes practice to develop the skill to make it go in the direction you want it to go.

The way you hold a Frisbee disc often determines the direction it will go. There are eight different ways to hold a Frisbee disc. Each grip is used for several different throws. For beginners, the thumb is held on top and the index finger is placed along the lip of the Frisbee disc. Fingers two, three and four are fanned out along the underside of the disc. With this basic grip, both the backhand and underhand throws can be done. As you practice with this grip, you may change it slightly to fit better your own style of throwing. There are several variations of the same grip that different champions have developed. Some have become famous for the unusual way they grip the Frisbee disc. As a beginner, however, you should stay with a proven grip. There will be plenty of time to develop your own style after you have learned the basics.

The basic grip.

The second basic grip is the two-finger grip. This grip gets its name from the position of two fingers on the underside of the disc. When using this grip, your Frisbee® disc will roll off the forefinger as it is released. The index finger braces against the forefingers.

Most throwers think of the forehand throw as the power throw. In the forehand throw, there is no follow through. The wrist action is most important. In preparing for the forehand throw, put your right hand out in front while turning it palm side up. Next, turn your arm clockwise as far as you can. Let your elbow come forward in front of your arm. Release the disc with a strong, quick flick of the wrist.

The two-finger grip.

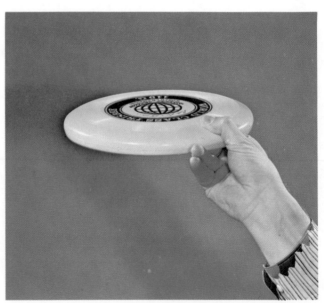

The forehand throw.

Behind-the-back throw.

Other throws that are done with this grip are the behind-the-back, behind-the-head and between-the-legs.

Between-the-legs throw.

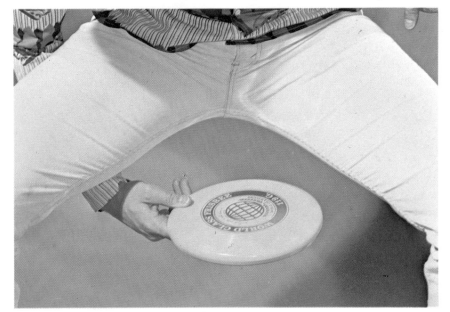

Another basic grip is the thumb grip. With this grip the Frisbee® disc comes off the thumb with a spin. The thumb is placed under the Frisbee disc while all four fingers are around the rim. This is a good grip for team competition since it makes the Frisbee disc hard to catch.

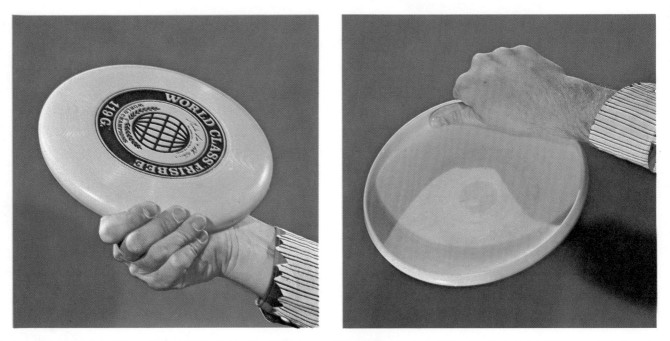

The thumb grip.

The overhand grip is almost like the thumb grip except the fingers are spread, not curled. It is a hard grip to learn, but a good one for power throws.

The overhand grip.

The last of the basic grips is called the hooked-thumb grip. It is the grip most often used for a back-hand throw. Place your thumb in a hooked position under the lip, all the way against the "cheek" of the Frisbee® disc. All four fingers should be curved around the slope of the other side.

The hooked thumb grip.

The five grips which have been explained are the basic grips needed to learn all of the known Frisbee® disc throws. The other three grips are trick-throwing grips which several of the champion throwers have worked out. These grips are not intended for power or distance. Their real purpose is for trick throws. They are the finger flip, the spider grip, and the hamburger grip. The hamburger grip is the only one of the grips which involves the use of both hands.

The finger grip.

The spider grip.

The hamburger grip.

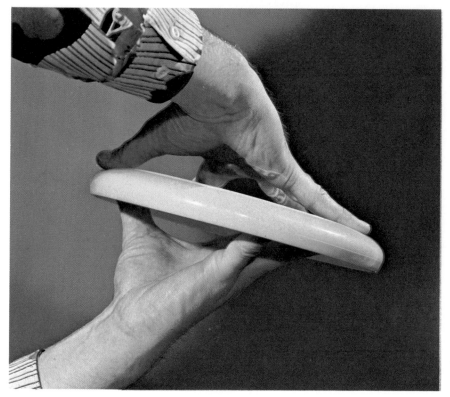

Knowing how to grip the Frisbee® disc for each throw is important. However, there is more to the throw than the grips which you may use. The whole body is involved in throwing the Frisbee disc. Running into the throw is necessary for a distance throw. The way you stand is important for accuracy. An accurate aim has to be developed through practice. Even what you do after the throw is important. This is called the followthrough. If you find that you are developing warps and wobbles in your throw, it is probably because your wrist action at the end of the throw doesn't make a good spin. This may cause the disc to go into a wobble soon after it is released. With practice, you will soon know how much spin to give. Next you will be ready to master such skills as hover flight, boomerangs, and skips.

Hovering the Frisbee disc is fun to do into the wind. It is often popular at the ocean. The hover is also a good throw to use if you are helping someone learn to catch a Frisbee disc. Since this flight is a slow one, it gives the person more time to position himself for the catch.

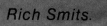

Rich Smits.

19

If you want to have fun with your Frisbee® disc when there is no one around to play with, try the boomerang throw. The first time you see this toss, you won't believe your eyes. It isn't easy. It's the mark of a master Frisbee disc thrower. Some of the tournament champions have practiced this throw so that they can stand in the same spot and the disc will return to them. This is one of the reasons they are champions.

The skip throw is another popular throw that takes a lot of practice. In a straight skip, the Frisbee disc bounces only once, usually about fifteen feet away. By adding a little curve to your skip throw, you may make it skip more than once. Both of these are done with an underhand toss.

The fingertip catch as demonstrated by John Kirkland and Jeff Jorgenson.

All of these special skills take practice. You won't be able to do any of these fancy throws the day you begin. Practicing throwing a Frisbee® disc isn't work. It's fun!

If you are going to have fun with other people and other Frisbee discs, you will have to learn to catch as well as throw. It's another game of give-and-take.

Frisbee disc throwers do not agree on whether it is better to catch the disc with thumbs up or thumbs down. Both sides try to explain their reasons in a scientific way. The beginner should do what comes naturally. If one way seems more comfortable, stay with it and practice. Either way, practice is the key.
good catch as it is to a good toss. As you wait for the catch, stand with your knees slightly bent so that you will be standing on the balls of your feet. Keep your eye on that flying disc and your body will go where your eye leads it. One of the things a beginner often does wrong is to reach too soon for the disc. Good timing, like everything else, comes with practice.

BASIC CATCHING POSITIONS

Thumbs down catch.

Thumbs up catch.

23

Gail McColl and Bill King make it look easy!

Frisbee® disc players who want to compete have organized tournaments throughout the country. The first tournament was held in Michigan in 1958. It developed a lot of interest in competition. More tournaments were organized in other parts of the country. Even winter weather was not a problem since some tournaments could be held indoors. Many college Frisbee disc teams held their own contests. Most of the other contests were open to anyone who could travel to the location of the tournament.

Many people's interest in Frisbee® disc competition led to the first World Frisbee® Championship which was held in 1968 at the Rose Bowl. Jay Shelton became the champion Frisbee disc thrower of the world. The next year Bob May became the new distance champ with a toss of 270 feet. The junior record was set that day by an eleven-year-old, Jeff Johnson. His winning throw was a distance of 165 feet.

By 1974, the Junior Frisbee® Tournament had become a big event. All the contestants were under fifteen years of age. There were different events that earned points for the winners. After all the contests, the contestant with the most points was the overall champion. If there was a tie, certain events were played again to break the tie. Some of the events included the distance throw, between-the-legs catch, behind-the-back catch, underhand skip, backhand skip, and many other skill throws and catches that take a lot of practice. World Champions don't just happen.

1977 WINNERS
INTERNATIONAL FRISBEE® CHAMPIONSHIPS

	MENS	WOMENS	SENIORS
OVERALL	John Kirkland	Monika Lou	Jack Roddick
DISTANCE	Joseph Youngmen	Monika Lou	Ken Van Sickle
ACCURACY	John Kirkland	Teresa Gaman	Jack Roddick
MAXIMUM TIME ALOFT	Dan Habeed	Monika Lou	Ed Headrick
THROW, RUN, CATCH	Joe Youngman	Jackie Entwistle	Jack Roddick
FRISBEE GOLF	Mark Horn	Marie Murphy	Jack Roddick
FREESTYLE	Jens & Erwin Velasquez	Monika Lou	Ralph Williamson

As contests began springing up everywhere, people in the International Frisbee® Association clubs started to think of more kinds of events for the contests. Many of these are individual events, but others are games that have made the Frisbee disc very popular.

The first known game to be played with Frisbee discs was called "Guts!" It can be played one-on-one or with any even number of players. The object of the game is to throw the Frisbee disc through the goal space so that no player on the other side can catch it. By doing this, the thrower scores. The catchers can score if the throwers toss a bad toss, such as out-of-bounds or a ground toss.

Erwin and Jens Velasquez in free style competition.

An ultimate game, Penn State vs. Santa Barbara.

Another game which is fast and fun is Street Frisbee®. The curbs on the street and the cracks in the surface form the boundaries. (Playing in the street can be dangerous, so be careful!) The object of the game is to stop the Frisbee disc behind the other team's goal before they can catch it. There are also many field games that are fun to play - Ultimate, Netbee, Courtsbee, Frisbee® Golf (Folf), Basebee, Frisbee® Football (Tiger), Horseshoe, Crossbee, and even Frisbee® Bowling. There seems to be no end to the fun that players can have with a Frisbee disc and a little imagination!

It is possible that no game of Frisbee® disc throwing will ever be invented which is as much fun as the games you play with your own dog and a Frisbee disc. Catching a Frisbee disc seems to be the most natural thing for a dog to do. A lot depends on the breed and disposition of your dog, but, chances are, your dog will want to learn to catch a Frisbee disc. With so many dogs enjoying the Frisbee disc, special tournaments have been developed for them. There is even an organization for them! It is called the K-9 Corps of the International Frisbee® Association. There are more than 300 dog members! One of the big names among them is Ashley Whippet. Since winning the national championship he has even appeared on the NFL halftime shows. He has become a favorite of many sports fans. There are other dogs who have made names for themselves and their owners by winning Frisbee disc tournaments.

There is even a special school for training dogs for such competitions. This school is called the Monterey Institute of Frisbee® Dog Studies, in Monterey, California.

The throw.

The catch.

If you would like to train your own dog to catch a Frisbee® disc there are some tips that may help. First, your dog should have his own Frisbee disc. It should be the right size for him, and should be the one you use every time you play with your dog. If your dog is one of the small breeds, his Frisbee disc should be the size of the Mini-Frisbee® disc which is smaller than the regular disc. For a medium breed dog, the regular Frisbee disc is just right. Larger dogs can handle the Pro Frisbee® disc or Master Frisbee® disc.

If you have already taught your dog to fetch, he will take to the flying disc idea quickly. If not, show him that it is his toy. Get him to chew on it. Roll it to him and encourage him to bring it back to you.

You and your dog can practice disc catching together by playing Dog-bee. All you need is your dog, his Frisbee disc, and an open place to run. The object of the game is to throw the disc so that the dog can catch it. His part of the game is to catch anything you can throw.

You can now see that there are many good reasons why we call the Frisbee® fabulous. Frisbee disc throwing is great fun as well as very good exercise. Throwing and catching the Frisbee disc developes good balance and coordination. If you are looking for excitement, go ahead, toss that Fabulous Frisbee®!

If you wish further information regarding this sport or its contests please contact:

The International Frisbee® Association
P.O. Box 970
San Gabriel, California 91776

This extremely difficult behind-the-back catch was completed to perfection by Gail McColl.